Florida Divorce Law Guide

ASHLEY D. BRUCE

CHRISTOPHER R. BRUCE

FLORIDA DIVORCE LAW GUIDE
Copyright © 2021 by Ashley & Christopher Bruce
All rights reserved.

Printed in the United States of America
First Printing, 2017

ISBN: 978-0-9975316-2-6

Ashley & Christopher Bruce
1601 Forum Place
Suite 1101
West Palm Beach, Florida 33401
12008 Southshore Boulevard
Suite 107
Wellington, Florida 33414

www.BrucePA.com

ACKNOWLEDGEMENTS

Thank you to our parents, Chrissy, Bernice, Russell, Spencer and Gernot. Your continued love, guidance, and encouragement makes us the world's luckiest children and has put us in the position of accomplishing anything we set our mind to achieving.

We are also especially grateful to those in the mental health profession who have trusted the attorneys of the Bruce Law Firm to help meet the marital and family law needs of their clients, while also helping our law firm's clients move on from the difficult experience of divorce (and sometimes avoid divorce completely through couple's therapy).

LEGAL DISCLAIMER

This book is about divorce planning and strategy and is not a legal treatise or dictionary. There are many lawyers, books and seminars which do an outstanding job explaining the numerous important intricacies of your state or country's divorce laws. Our advice is to hire a competent and ethical divorce lawyer to help you understand how the laws of your state or country apply to your specific situation and to help refine the goals and strategies we tell you to implement in this book. The explanations about divorce law and strategy in this book are not a substitute for hiring a competent divorce lawyer, which is what we recommend you do.

TABLE OF CONTENTS

INTRODUCTION...i

   Other Resources Designed to Help You iii

Learn What Is Important About Divorce Laws....................1

   Why You Need to Know the Basic Fundamentals of the Relevant Law 3

   The Basics of Dividing Property & Debts.................................7

   The Basics of Valuing a Business or Professional Practice 15

   The Basics of Alimony 22

   The Basics of Child Custody 31

   The Basics of Child Support 41

   The Basics of Attorney's Fee & Cost Sharing Laws...........................45

   The Basics of Enforcing & Challenging Prenuptial Agreements..........52

   The Basics of Several Other Legal Issues.................................59

Learn What Is Important About the Divorce Court Process & Timing..65

   Why You Need to Know About the Legal Process 67

   The Divorce Lawsuit Filing & Responses 69

   The Initial Exchange of Financial Records.................................73

   Settling Your Divorce Through Mediation 78

   A Word About Collaborative Law/Divorce.................................83

   The Uncontested Final Hearing & Final Judgment...........................86

   Temporary Relief Hearings 89

   Depositions 93

   Trial 96

   Divorce Court Appeals 99

Our Other Books Designed to Help You 102

ABOUT THE AUTHORS 104

INTRODUCTION

We are divorce lawyers. You'd probably be surprised to know that, despite our profession, we are not personally a fan of divorce and everything that comes with it. For this reason, we created the website www.StayMarriedFlorida.com to help people avoid divorce (more on that soon). That said, we believe there is a time and a place for divorce. For some people, the only way to live a happy, healthy and productive life is to end their marriage. These are the people we help in our law practice.

We've written several books on divorce and divorce strategy. These books are available for free download at www.DivorceInformationBooks.com. This particular book focuses on what you need to know about Florida's Divorce Laws, and the Florida Divorce Court process.

When you expect a difficult divorce, or even a simple divorce, it is it is critical to know the basics of the relevant laws that will apply to your situation. If you have a basic idea of the relevant laws it will be easier for you to know is possible (and not possible) in your divorce. This is important, because "what is possible" in your divorce is a driving force behind settlement negotiations, and also allows you to be in a position of knowing when your spouse is misleading you about how Florida's divorce laws work.

In addition to knowing the basics of the relevant divorce laws, it is also important for you to know "what will happen" and "when it is going to happen" once your divorce lawsuit starts in the legal system. This is all covered in the second section of this book. Once you know this, you'll know what to expect during the legal process, and in my experience, be more at ease as you contemplate divorce.

Divorce is not always easy, or comfortable, but it is much better when the legal rules and processes are de-mystified and understood. We hope this book helps you feel more confident in your situation and we wish you the best as you continue to educate yourself about this process.

Ashley & Christopher Bruce
West Palm Beach, Florida

Other Resources Designed to Help You

Before we go any further, we wanted to make a quick mention of resources we've put online to further help you navigate the divorce process. Our law firm's website, **www.BrucePA.com**, has complementary books, seminars, and forums on divorce strategy, law, and procedure. Also, there are several books available for free download at www.DivorceInformationBooks.com. These books are free and include the Women's Guide for Getting Organized for Divorce, How to Divorce Your Controlling, Manipulative, Narcissistic Husband, our guide on How to Find & Hire Your Divorce Lawyer, and Control Your Difficult Divorce, our comprehensive divorce strategy guide.

Also, because it is our belief that the real best divorce is the divorce that didn't have to happen, the Bruce Law Firm developed and supports www.StayMarriedFlorida.com, a website devoted to helping couples build, have, and keep healthy relationships. The website has articles, podcast interviews, and a growing directory of extremely talented results-driven therapists.

Learn What Is Important About Divorce Laws

Why You Need to Know the Basic Fundamentals of the Relevant Law

Like it or not, you are living in a nation "built upon the rule of law." This means that you need to develop a *Best Divorce* strategy that takes into account the laws that will govern your divorce if you want to have the *Best Divorce* possible. You are setting yourself up for failure if you fail to educate yourself about what is important about the law. Doing so is the equivalent of taking a medication without knowing its side effects or planning a once in a lifetime vacation without looking at a map to see if there is a road, boat, or jet that can get you where you want to go. We doubt you've ever made important life choices without regard to the potential outcomes or any analysis as to whether your goals are possible. Your divorce should be no different.

Fortunately, you can skip learning 99.99% of what lawyers study in law school, and at this point, just focus on the basics of what will be relevant to your divorce. We say the basics, because right now, all you should be doing is obtaining a general education about how the law works as you begin to develop your *Best Divorce* strategy (for more on how to develop a divorce strategy, view the Bruce Law Firm's book, Control Your Difficult Divorce, which is available for free download at www.ControlYourDifficultDivorce.com).

Down the line, once you have learned the basics about the law, there will be a time for you to develop, with the help of your lawyer, an in-depth understanding of any subtle intricacies in the law applicable to your specific situation.

In many instances, there is not going to be a novel legal issue involved with your divorce case. Most of the disagreements, if any, will likely involve tussles over establishing facts (such as the value of an asset or the amount of someone's actual or potential income). As such, your devotion to learning all of the details of the law that competent divorce lawyers spend years acquiring is going to likely be overwhelming, mind-numbing, and not worth any incremental benefit justifying the effort.

Our recommendation is to first learn the general basics of the applicable law as covered in this section of the book. As you go through the material, you should make a note of any questions that come up specific to your situation. You will then cover these issues shortly down the line when you consult with a divorce lawyer and refine your divorce strategy (on that note, you can get the Bruce Law Firm's book on How to Find, Hire, & Work With Your Divorce Lawyer at www.AllAboutDivorceLawyers.com).

As you are reading the material that follows in this section, you need to know that divorce laws are jurisdiction and state-specific. Although most countries and states have similar laws, there are some differences. We are divorce lawyers in Florida, so in some cases, the explanation that follows is geared to Florida Law that is usually, but not always, consistent with the laws in most other places.

We note that we've written the material that follows as generally as possible, for the purpose of allowing you to develop the appropriate baseline level of knowledge we believe you need to have at this point, as you are working up to developing your goals for your divorce, and ultimately developing a divorce strategy in consultation with a competent divorce lawyer. With this being the case, you should consult with an experienced divorce lawyer familiar with the law in your jurisdiction, before taking action in your divorce.

What follows is an explanation of the basics of how the law works with the topics that come up most often in a divorce. While we've made every best effort to use an entertaining writing style and to speak in plain English, instead of using legal jargon, if you are falling asleep reading this chapter you can always take the easy way out and consult with an experienced divorce lawyer who can probably tell you what you need to know in a one-hour office meeting. That said, you can get through this section of the book quicker than it takes to find a good lawyer and drive to their office. Out of risk of delaying cash flow to our profession, our recommendation is to read on and save the lawyers for a little bit later (you'll probably have enough of lawyers soon anyway…).

The Basics of Dividing Property & Debts

This section covers the general basics of how the law usually works when it comes to dividing the things you own and the money you owe with your spouse. The next chapter goes in more detail about how your business is addressed in divorce, and is therefore not mentioned below.

The bottom line under the law is that, with few exceptions, you and your spouse should each receive one half of the "marital net worth" in your divorce. This means that you should get an amount of money, property, and debt that is equal to half the value of all "marital assets" minus all "marital liabilities."

Notably, "marital assets" and "marital liabilities" usually will not include (1) assets inherited during the marriage that are always kept separate; (2) property owned prior to the marriage; or (3) liabilities that preexisted or were unrelated to the marriage. Such assets and liabilities are referred to as "non-marital" and are kept out of what is the usually equal division of "marital net worth" in a divorce.

By way of example, assume the following facts:

1. Your "marital assets" are worth two million dollars;

2. Your "marital liabilities" total one million dollars; and

3. Right before the divorce started, you inherited one million dollars that you deposited into a separate bank account and never mixed with any "marital assets."

Under these facts, there would be a "marital net worth" of one million dollars ($2,000,000 in marital assets - $1,000,000 in marital liabilities = $1,000,000 marital net worth). In your divorce, you and your spouse would each leave the marriage with a "marital net worth" equal to five hundred thousand dollars ($1,000,000 "marital net worth" x 50% = $500,000 "marital net worth" for each spouse). Further, you would also keep your one-million-dollar inheritance, which is not a marital asset since you always kept it separate. After everything is said and done, your net worth after the divorce will be $1.5 million (your $500,000 share of the "marital net worth" + your $1,000,000 inheritance= $1,500,000).

Usually, each individual asset and liability is not literally split equally. Instead, each person will receive certain assets and liabilities, so that each spouse leaves the marriage with approximately the same "marital net worth." In certain situations, where most of the "marital net worth" is tied up in a house or business, it may be necessary for assets to be sold, or for one spouse to make payments to the other over time in order for each spouse to have an equal "marital net worth" after the divorce.

Dividing property sounds simple in principle. It can be, but there can also be complications. Most of the squabbling/litigation with dividing property is over: (1) determining the value of an asset; (2) determining the date used to identify and value an marital assets/liabilities; (3) determining whether an asset/liability is "marital" or "non-marital"; (4) determining whether there is any "equitable basis" for one spouse to receive an "unequal" amount of the marital assets/liabilities; and (5) determining whether either spouse wrongfully secreted "marital assets" or wrongfully incurred "marital liabilities." These sub-issues of dividing property and debt in divorce are explained further below.

Determining the value of an asset:

While it is simple to figure out the value of a bank account or credit card debt by looking at the appropriate financial statements, other assets are not as easy to value and necessitate a forensic accountant or appraiser for a more definite valuation. This is especially the case with businesses, which are covered in more depth in the next chapter. Valuation issues requiring an appraiser also commonly come up when the marital assets include real estate, alternative investments, yachts, jewelry, art, and other collectibles. Although you may feel like the costs of the lawyers are already high enough for you to pay, it can be worth your money to obtain appraisals on the value of any unique marital asset to ensure you are not shorting yourself in a settlement by placing too high or low of a value on an asset.

Determining the date for identifying and valuing marital assets/liabilities:

Contrary to general thinking, in many jurisdictions (including Florida), an asset or liability is "presumed" to be "marital" if it existed on the date the divorce was filed, with the date for identifying marital assets/liabilities usually being the "filing date" of the divorce. Many people are shocked to learn that assets/liabilities that accumulate during long periods of separation can be "marital," even when a spouse has moved on and is living with a separate person. As far as the "valuation date," most assets are valued as of the date the divorce was filed. However, a value closer to trial will usually be used for assets with values that passively increase/decrease due to market forces and not the efforts of any spouse (such as an investment in a stock market index fund that rises and falls with the stock market). The date closest to trial will also be used to value an asset in most cases, if a spouse was forced to spend down the value of an asset during the divorce case, to support themselves, their spouse, or pay the costs of litigation.

Determining whether an asset is "marital" or "non-marital":

Generally speaking, an asset is "non-marital" if it was owned prior to the marriage or inherited, as long as the asset was always kept separate from "marital assets." That said, there is usually a "rebuttable presumption" that all assets or liabilities owned by either spouse are "marital" in nature and part of the usually equal division of the "marital net worth" upon divorce. In other words, all assets and liabilities are "marital" unless someone proves they are "non-marital," which can be easier said than done if the person with the burden of proof is you. Complicating this issue are the concepts of "comingling" and "marital improvements." Under the "comingling" concept; if a "non-marital" money is mixed with "marital" money, then the "non-marital" money is usually converted into a marital asset (meaning you have to split it with your spouse). Under the "marital improvements" concept; the amount of an increase in value of a "non-marital" asset that can be (1) traced to your efforts during the marriage or (2) the expenditure of marital funds, is a "marital asset" subject to division.

All of this can start to get complicated if you inherited money during the marriage or brought assets into the marriage that had any significant value. If this is the case, you would be well served by obtaining as many details as you can about your inheritance or assets owned prior to the marriage, including: (1) when you first obtained the asset; (2) what happened to the asset during the marriage (was it kept separate, mixed with other assets, etc.); (3) how did the value change during the marriage; and (4) is any change in value possibly attributable to your efforts during the marriage or the expenditure of marital funds. Then, discuss these details when you consult with an attorney.

Determining if there should be an "unequal distribution" of the "marital net worth":

In most jurisdictions, the divorce judge has the ability to determine whether there should be an unequal division of the "marital net worth." In other words, the judge could determine you will receive less than fifty percent of the "marital net worth." While most jurisdictions allow for this "unequal distribution" in theory, in practice, this can be extremely difficult to convince a divorce court judge (who is used to dividing marital assets equally) to implement anything other than an equal split of the "marital net worth" unless part of the net worth is made up of what used to be non-marital assets.

In case you were wondering, the "my spouse had an affair" or "my spouse was lazy the entire marriage while I worked 80 hours a week" arguments, will almost never be enough to convince a judge to depart far from the typical "fifty-fifty" division of the "marital net worth." Usually, there has to be an exceptional circumstance to justify an "unequal distribution" of the "marital net worth."

Determining whether there was "wrongful dissipation":

"Wrongful dissipation" occurs when it is proven that one spouse spent down assets or incurred liabilities on an affair, or another purpose deemed "unrelated to the marriage." If "wrongful dissipation" is proven, then the other spouse will receive a credit for half the amount that was wrongfully dissipated. The credit is half the amount of "wrongful dissipation", because the non-offending spouse would have otherwise received one half of each dollar that was dissipated.

By way of example, assume (1) each spouse was set to receive $500,000 as their half of the "marital net worth" and (2) it was proven that the husband wrongfully dissipated $100,000. Under these facts, the wife would receive $550,000 (her $500,000 share of the marital assets plus half of the $100,000 that the husband wrongfully dissipated) and the husband would receive $450,000 of marital net worth in the divorce (his $500,000 share of the marital assets minus half of the $100,000 that he wrongfully dissipated).

The Basics of Valuing a Business or Professional Practice

For many of our clients, the issue of "how do we deal with the business" is one of the most important issues to address in their divorce. This chapter covers several topics relevant to valuing a business or professional practice in divorce, and the principles below are equally applicable to active and passive investments made in business entities that are not publicly traded (including partnerships, joint ventures, etc.). If you or your spouse do not operate a business or hold an interest in an investment partnership or other entity then you can skim or skip this chapter altogether.

A business or professional practice must be made part of the division of property upon divorce, along with all of the other marital property. However, in many instances, determining the value of a business requires more than simply looking at bank accounts and balance sheets, and requires a more in-depth analysis of the company's general ledgers, check registers, inventory, and in some instances, particular knowledge of the industry in which the business operates. This is where a divorce attorney with an accounting background can come in handy. But, even if your lawyer enjoys burying themselves in spreadsheets, you will likely need to hire a forensic accountant experienced in divorce accounting, and in some instances specialized appraisers, to assist your lawyer in determining the appropriate valuation for your business. More information on this is available in the chapter titled *Forensic Accountants & Other Experts* in the Bruce Law Firm's Book titled How to Find, Hire, & Work With Your Divorce Lawyer (available for free download at www.AllAboutDivorceLawyers.com).

The most common issues relevant to handling and valuing a business or professional practice in a divorce are: (1) who gets the business/practice in the divorce; (2) what is the valuation method used; and (3) does the value of the business include a "goodwill/reputation value."

Who gets the business in the divorce?

Divorce court judges are usually inclined to allow the spouse that ran the business during the marriage to keep the business after the divorce. If both spouses were involved in the business, then the judge is likely to find a way to keep them from being in business with each other after the marriage is over. If you ran the business during the marriage, and your spouse's role was nonexistent or strictly administrative in nature, then you will likely keep control of your business in the divorce. Similarly, if the business is a professional practice such as a law firm or medical office, the spouse who is the professional is going to keep the business. If the business has other partners/shareholders besides you and your spouse, then the judge is more likely to award the marital shares in the business to the spouse that has a best likelihood of maintaining control over the enterprise in the future. Judges try to avoid situations where a former spouse ends up having their business interest effectively rendered worthless by corporate bully tactics of other shareholders aligning with one spouse over another.

The valuation method:

Many businesses will be valued based on a "net book value valuation." This means that the value of the business for purposes of the divorce will be the value of the company's assets minus its liabilities. In most other instances, an "enterprise" value can be given to the business, which is more reflective of the price a willing buyer would pay for the business. The difference between which valuation method is used typically depends on whether the company's "goodwill" is to be part of the value, which is an issue explained in the next section below. Regardless of which valuation method is used, there can be a great deal of time spent determining the value of a company's assets or liabilities, as each line item of a balance sheet is subject to manipulation/speculation. This is especially the case with determining the appropriate value of a company's inventory, accounts receivable, and property/plant/equipment line items, as the true fair market value of these items is often different than the depreciated values reported for tax purposes and internal reporting. In some instances, especially when the business houses inventory or has operations requiring the use of specialized, expensive equipment, the valuation of the business ends up becoming a compilation of multiple "mini-valuations" of the major aspects on the company balance sheet.

Is there "goodwill/reputation value?

The issue of whether a "goodwill/reputation value" is included in the value of a business is critical, because the character of a business' goodwill determines the methodology used for valuing the business in a divorce. With few exceptions, when a "personal goodwill case" is identified, the valuation of the business is much simpler, especially in cases where the inventory or other assets of the business do not present any unique valuation issue. In most situations, the upfront identification of "personal goodwill cases" makes it easier for the parties to agree upon a value of a business without devoting significant resources towards a full-blown business evaluation.

Personal goodwill is goodwill attributable to the skill, reputation, and continued participation of a spouse in a business. This is most common with professional practices, where the entire value of the business is riding on the reputation of the lawyer, doctor, or other professional who is the primary revenue generator. In most jurisdictions, personal "goodwill" or "reputation value" must be excluded when assigning a value to a business. The theory behind this is that any value that attaches to a business as a result of personal goodwill/reputation, represents nothing more than a spouse's probable future earning capacity, which is not awarded in a divorce. Divorces involving a professional practice, such as a legal or accounting practice, almost always represent "personal goodwill cases."

With many professional practices, the business valuation is relatively simple. The company's value will primarily consist of the money in the company bank accounts, accounts receivable, accounts payable, and the whatever fair market value there is to the assets of the practice (the desks, computers and the outdated phone system).

Enterprise goodwill is defined as the value of a business "which exceeds its tangible assets" and represents "the tendency of clients/patients to return to and recommend the practice irrespective of the reputation of the individual practitioner." Unlike personal goodwill, enterprise goodwill is included in the value of the business for purposes of divorce. A classic example of enterprise goodwill would be the goodwill associated with a food or automobile franchise. With these businesses, most consumers will frequent the business due to the reputation of the product/brand, and not the name of the franchisee.

The distinction between "personal goodwill cases" and "enterprise goodwill cases" can seem harder to determine in some businesses, especially quasi-franchise type businesses. A classic example would be the valuation of the branded dental and healthcare clinics that now occupy office space everywhere, or other businesses where some but not all of a customer base is drawn to a business because of the reputation of its owner. The key to determining whether the goodwill is personal goodwill or enterprise goodwill in these "close call" cases, is the necessity or existence of a covenant not to compete if the business is sold. At least in Florida, the goodwill of a business associated with the owner executing a legitimate covenant not to compete is considered personal goodwill that isn't valued in the divorce.

The Basics of Alimony

Alimony is the term given to financial support paid, usually monthly, from one former spouse to another after the marriage is over. Alimony is a "creature of statute" and the rules regarding it differ greatly between jurisdictions. Some jurisdictions use a mathematical formula to determine the amount of alimony. However in Florida, the law puts certain limitations on alimony but otherwise leaves the exact determination of the amount and duration of alimony largely to the discretion of divorce court judges.

Generally speaking, two facts must be established before a judge orders the payment of alimony: (1) one spouse must actually need financial support from the other spouse to pay their living expenses after maximizing their earning potential and (2) the other spouse must actually have the financial ability to pay financial support to the other party in addition to their own reasonable living expenses. Although this seems simple in concept, the amount and duration of alimony is one of the most contentious issues in divorce litigation. This is for good reason, as the amount of alimony paid or received can be the difference between both the spouse paying or receiving the alimony being comfortable after the divorce or living in the proverbial "poor house."

The most contested issues that come up concerning alimony are typically: (1) determining each spouse's income for evaluating how much alimony they need or can pay; (2) determining the "standard of living" the alimony analysis is based on; (3) determining how much alimony will be awarded; (4) determining how long alimony is paid; (5) determining when alimony can be changed or stopped completely; and (6) determining what happens if someone stops paying alimony.

Determining income for the alimony analysis:

Determining the income of the spouse paying and receiving alimony is a critical component to determining how much alimony one spouse needs, and what the other spouse is capable of paying. In a perfect world, both spouses would be employees with a long, demonstrated earnings record. In practice, however, this is rarely the case when alimony is being contested. This is because, in many cases, when the spouse requesting alimony has not worked in a long time, there is an issue of how much money, if any, they can or should have to earn to contribute to their own support needs. Further, in many cases where enough money is made for a spouse to stay home, the other spouse is self-employed. This often means their true cash flow available for paying alimony is different than their income reported for tax purposes.

Judges typically determine a spouse's need for alimony after considering how much money the spouse could make if their employment potential is maximized. This means that if a spouse is not working, but could work, the judge will need to determine how much the spouse could earn if they were to re-enter the workforce. Similarly, if the spouse is not maximizing their education and training in their current job, a judge could determine that they are capable of earning more if presented with appropriate evidence.

When a spouse's earning capacity is contested, it is sometimes the case that a vocational expert will be brought in to determine how much the spouse could earn if they maximized their employability. There are numerous rules and boundaries surrounding this fact intensive analysis, which will need to be explained by an attorney in your jurisdiction. But the bottom line is that the alimony needs analysis will usually be based on a spouse's potential (not actual) income if they are physically capable of working, but are currently unemployed or underemployed.

Likewise, a self-employed spouse's income for determining their ability to pay alimony is not as simple as using the income figure that appears on a tax return or profit and loss statement. In many cases when the spouse who will pay alimony is a business owner or is otherwise self-employed, there must be an analysis of how much cash flow the spouse receives from the business.

A good part of the work in many divorce cases is putting a number on the amount of the fringe benefits and in-kind benefits that a spouse receives from their business that are not included in their reported taxable income. As an example, businesses commonly pay for vacations, automobiles, and other fringe benefits of the owner. These types of expenses must be quantified and added back to the owner-spouse's reported income to determine the spouse's "divorce court income" available for paying alimony.

**Determining the "standard of living" for the alimony analysis**:

The law typically makes the marital standard of living the starting point for determining a spouse's needs for financial support after the divorce. As an example, if the marital standard of living was to live in a one-million-dollar house, drive foreign cars, take luxurious vacations, and send the kids to private school, then the measuring of a spouse's financial need for alimony after the divorce will usually be based on the costs of continuing a similar lifestyle after the divorce. By implication, spouses who historically lived financially frugal lifestyles, will have a lower standard of living, and all factors being equal, would receive less alimony than a spouse from a marriage earning the same annual income but having lower expenses.

When people cannot agree, the actual dollar amount of a spouse's need for alimony is determined by having an accountant preform a "needs analysis," which is a one to two-year study of how much spouses spent on each category of expenses, with certain adjustments made to reflect necessary changes in lifestyle after the divorce. It should be noted that while the standard of living during the marriage is usually the starting point for determining a spouse's need for financial support, there are some exceptions to this that vary by jurisdiction. In many cases, the standard of living during the marriage becomes less relevant to the alimony analysis in shorter marriages or in marriages where the couple lived beyond their financial means.

Determining the amount of alimony:

With several notable exceptions and limitations, the amount of alimony is typically a mathematical function of (1) the cost for the spouse to live after the divorce (which is typically based on the marital standard of living) minus (2) the amount of money the spouse seeking alimony can earn if maximizing their employment potential. By way of example, if a spouse seeking alimony will have expenses of $5,000/month after the divorce and is capable of earning $4,000/month by maximizing their employment potential, then the amount of alimony would be $1,000/month. Remember as stated above that alimony is only ordered paid if the spouse requesting alimony actually needs financial support. There will be no alimony paid if it is proven that the spouse seeking alimony is capable of paying their after-divorce living expenses out of their income.

Further, alimony typically cannot be awarded in an amount that leaves the spouse paying alimony with less cash flow than the spouse receiving alimony. Also, in jurisdictions where alimony is not determined by a formula, there are usually some customary "rules of thumb" maximums for alimony. As an example, in Florida alimony will rarely exceed 40% of the gross income of the spouse paying alimony in long term marriages, and in marriages lasting less than seven years the amount of alimony will usually not exceed 20% of the gross income of the spouse paying alimony. The bottom line is that you need to speak with an attorney in your local area to get a better feel for what type of alimony you might realistically expect to pay or receive, as the amount can vary by jurisdiction and between judges.

Determining how long alimony will be paid:

The length of time the alimony payments last depends on the specifics of the support needed, but will vary significantly between courthouses and judges, which is why some states base the duration upon statutory formulas. Sometimes, the alimony will stop after a period of time deemed necessary for the spouse to become self-supporting. In other cases, the alimony will be paid over a much longer duration.

As a rule of thumb, alimony is usually not going to be longer than half the length of the marriage in marriages lasting less than ten years, but as the marriage gets longer, the duration the alimony payments last typically extends. Although "permanent alimony" still exists in many states, the term is somewhat of a misnomer. As explained below, alimony payments usually stop once the person paying alimony gets to retirement age, or upon other major life events.

Determining when alimony payments change or stop completely:

It is almost always the case that alimony payments terminate upon either spouse's death or upon the alimony recipient getting remarried, or in some cases, cohabitating. Further, most jurisdictions have laws allowing alimony to be reduced or terminated upon the person paying alimony reaching a reasonable retirement age and actually retiring. Otherwise, most jurisdictions have laws allowing alimony to increase or decrease upon a showing of a substantial, unanticipated, change in circumstances, such as losing a job or suffering a health condition that increases their need for alimony or ability to pay alimony.

Although, in theory, alimony is almost always subject to change, be mindful that in practice, it is burdensome and expensive to change the amount of alimony. For this reason, it is critical to ensure the original alimony award is realistic and sufficient when your case is settled. It is asking for trouble to agree to an unrealistic or insufficient alimony award with the thought that you will simply go and change alimony later.

Consequences of not paying alimony:

Most jurisdictions have laws designed to encourage people to

pay the alimony set in their divorce. The bottom line is spouses who refuse to pay alimony despite having the ability to make the payments risk going to jail in addition to having their wages garnished and assets levied.

The Basics of Child Custody

The issue of "who gets the children" can be one of the most sensitive and awful aspects of divorce. The laws regarding child custody (also called timesharing) can vary widely between jurisdictions and application of the laws can vary widely within the same jurisdiction as judges typically have great "discretion" to make decisions about children. A thorough explanation of the strategy for handling contested custody litigation, especially parental alienation cases, would fill a book of its own.

If you have or anticipate a seriously contested issue involving children (meaning you are being kept from a child or your spouse has serious flaws that make you believe they should be kept from a child) then you need to make it a priority to consult with an experienced divorce lawyer familiar with how your local judges approach child custody cases now. Read the Bruce Law Firm's book on how to find, hire, and work with your divorce lawyer, which is available for free download at www.AllAboutDivorceLawyers.com.

Judges seem to have a habit of leaving parents in the situation created by the decisions they made before becoming heavily entrenched in custody litigation. For this reason, it is critical that your early decisions are the right decisions based on your long-term goals.

Scary warnings aside, for most people, there is nothing substantial to worry about when it comes to the children. We regularly tell clients in Palm Beach County, Florida, where we primarily practice, that many of our local judges start from the position that each parent should have an equal amount of time with their children, if they are a safe person and actually have the interest of being with their children half the time.

Many judges have had experience in juvenile or dependency court before they are made a divorce court judge. After seeing what happens to children who don't have any parents, these judges are usually starting from the position that both parents should spend equal time with their children, and be equally involved in parenting decisions, unless there is a really good reason for this to not be the case.

In many cases, at least here in Palm Beach County, the "worst case" scenario for a parent who has proven to be a safe person and productive member of society, is for the judge to implement a "model" schedule that has the children spending days and nights with both parents during the week, and dividing all major holidays in an equal manner that rotates between the parents each year. This "worst case" scenario schedule works out to one parent having about 62% of the time and the other parent having about 38% of the time with the children.

The fact that this "worst case" scenario often leaves the parent receiving the "38% of the time" portion of the schedule with more quality time with their children than they had during the marriage, and more time than they can realistically manage with a busy work schedule, usually operates to get most parents to agree to issues involving their children and keep them out of court.

Many clients who consult with us and have children usually ask us some variation of "who is going to get custody of the kids?" we end up explaining that in Florida, the term "custody" is outdated and almost never applicable. In 2008, Florida's laws were changed to eliminate the term "custody" from most statutes. Now, down here in the "Sunshine State," the issues to decide in a child custody case are "timesharing" and "parental responsibility." "Timesharing," is the term used to describe how parents share time with the children, and "parental responsibility" is the term used to describe how parents make decisions for the children. Many other jurisdictions have made similar changes to their laws, or have at least legally "neutered" the legal effect of "having custody" to the point of being meaningless.

As it relates to "timesharing," in Florida (and in many other jurisdictions) it is now the case that there is no presumption that a child should spend more time with their mother or with their father. It used to be the case that a legal doctrine called the "tender years doctrine" applied and dictated that children should spend their early years primarily with their mother. However, it has been over twenty-five years now since the Florida Supreme Court pronounced the "tender years doctrine" as "dead." As a result, in theory, judges should set timesharing/visitation schedules based on evaluations of the decision-making criteria listed in the custody laws (explained at the end of this section below) without regard to the sex of the parent.

The practical effect of all of this is that most judges are predisposed to leaving similarly situated parents with an equal amount of timesharing/visitation with their children after a divorce. This means that if both spouses are capable parents and have similar availability to be with the children, many judges are likely to implement an equal timesharing/visitation schedule.

This, of course, varies between judges, and in our experience, results in newer judges being almost dead set on putting in place a 50-50 timesharing/visitation schedule, and more experienced judges sometimes believing the children should spend more time with their mother.

Further, if one parent has been a stay-at-home parent during the marriage while the other parent has been working 80 hours a week, judges are likely to fashion a different schedule (in Palm Beach County, this is likely to be the 62%/38% "model schedule" described above). Also, as common sense would dictate, this all changes if one parent has a serious substance abuse problem, mental health issue, or other issues that makes it unsafe for them to be around the children. If danger to the children is proven, judges can and will limit or eliminate the problem parent's access to the children.

The issue of "parental responsibility," covers how parents make educational, health, religious, and other important decisions for their children. As with timesharing, in Florida and in many other jurisdictions, the law is usually set up for these decisions to be shared equally, or close to equally. As an example, in Florida, the law is set up to presume that parents should, by default, have what is called "shared parental responsibility." This means that the parents are supposed to be jointly responsible for making all important decisions for their children (we're talking about decisions on important, long lasting issues and not decisions on day-to-day issues like what a child eats for breakfast). In Florida, judges are required to order "shared parental responsibility," unless there is evidence that doing so will be detrimental to the child, which is extremely hard to prove.

The bottom line to all of this is, in many jurisdictions, if you and your spouse are generally good, safe adults, who have been historically involved with your children, then after the divorce, you are likely going to have an equal say in the important decisions for the children, and will probably have equal or close to equal amount of time with them.

That said, you need to speak to a lawyer immediately if your spouse is jerking you around with the children, has threatened to cause problems involving the children, or is unsafe to be around the children. If there is an anticipated complication involving your relationship with your children, you need to make sure it is handled correctly from the very beginning, or you will jeopardize your children's upbringing and the quality of your lifetime relationship with them. This might be the only thing left that is really important to you after your marriage is over, especially in the future when the divorce is all but forgotten.

For those who are interested, we have listed below the major factors below that Florida judges are required to consider when deciding "timesharing" and "parental responsibility" issues for children. The laws of many other jurisdictions require judges to analyze similar factors when deciding contested child custody cases. If you feel you have learned enough about child custody laws for now, then you can move on to the next chapter.

Custody Factors:

a. The demonstrated capacity and disposition of each parent, to facilitate and encourage a close and continuing parent-child relationship, to honor the time-sharing schedule, and to be reasonable when changes are required.

b. The anticipated division of parental responsibilities after the litigation, including the extent to which parental responsibilities will be delegated to third parties.

c. The demonstrated capacity and disposition of each parent to determine, consider, and act upon the needs of the child as opposed to the needs or desires of the parent.

d. The length of time the child has lived in a stable, satisfactory environment and the desirability of maintaining continuity.

e. The geographic viability of the parenting plan, with special attention paid to the needs of school-age children and the amount of time to be spent traveling to effectuate the parenting plan. This factor does not create a presumption for or against relocation of either parent with a child.

f. The moral fitness of the parents.

g. The mental and physical health of the parents.

h. The home, school and community record of the child.

i. The reasonable preference of the child, if the court deems the child to be of sufficient intelligence, understanding, and experience to express a preference.

j. The demonstrated knowledge, capacity, and disposition of each parent to be informed of the circumstances of the minor child, including, but not limited to, the child's friends, teachers, medical care providers, daily activities, and favorite things.

k. The demonstrated capacity and disposition of each parent to provide a consistent routine for the child, such as discipline, and daily schedules for homework, meals, and bedtime.

l. The demonstrated capacity of each parent to communicate with and keep the other parent informed of issues and activities regarding the minor child, and the willingness of each parent to adopt a unified front on all major issues when dealing with the child.

m. Evidence of domestic violence, sexual violence, child abuse, child abandonment, or child neglect, regardless of whether a prior or pending action relating to those issues has been brought. If the court accepts evidence of prior or pending actions regarding domestic violence, sexual violence, child abuse, child abandonment, or child neglect, the court must specifically acknowledge in writing that such evidence was considered when evaluating the best interests of the child.

n. Evidence that either parent has knowingly provided false information to the court, regarding any prior or pending action regarding domestic violence, sexual violence, child abuse, child abandonment, or child neglect.

o. The particular parenting tasks customarily performed by each parent, and the division of parental responsibilities before the institution of litigation and during the pending litigation, including the extent to which parenting responsibilities were undertaken by third parties.

p. The demonstrated capacity and disposition of each parent to participate and be involved in the child's school and extracurricular activities.

q. The demonstrated capacity and disposition of each parent to maintain an environment for the child which is free from substance abuse.

r. The capacity and disposition of each parent to protect the child from the ongoing litigation as demonstrated by not discussing the litigation with the child, not sharing documents or electronic media related to the litigation with the child, and refraining from disparaging comments about the other parent to the child.

s. The developmental stages and needs of the child and the demonstrated capacity and disposition of each parent to meet the child's developmental needs.

t. Any other factor that is relevant to the determination of a specific parenting plan, including the time-sharing schedule.

The Basics of Child Support

Child support is usually a fairly straightforward matter compared to the other legal issues that come up in a divorce lawsuit. In Florida, and in many other jurisdictions, child support is based on a formula that is primarily controlled by: (1) each parent's income from all sources, including employment, alimony received, and passive income from investments; (2) the number of nights each parent spends with the children a year; and (3) a few expenses related to the children, such as health insurance and reasonable expenses for childcare. With very few exceptions that almost never apply, child support is determined by this child support formula and the number "is what it is" and cannot be avoided.

Theoretically speaking, the formula usually makes sense. Through the formula the very basic costs of caring for children (as determined by the infinite wisdom of your government) is spread between both parents based on their relative incomes, how much time they spend with the kids, and who pays how much for the major expenses of insurance and childcare. In the perfect (seemingly imaginary) world where each parent's income, time with the children, and out of pocket payments for children's expenses are equal, then there will not be child support.

As with alimony, child support is based on the income that a person should be making after using their best efforts to find the highest paying employment available. This means that you cannot "beat the system" by refusing to work, solely for the purpose of paying less (or receiving more) in child support. Also, similar to with alimony, if you are a business owner or are self-employed, you can count on your spouse's divorce lawyer doing whatever they can to show that your income, for purposes of calculating child support, should be higher than your reported taxable income, by re-characterizing certain business expenses that are really personal benefits as income to you.

In Florida, there is a doctrine dealing with "good fortune child support" that was derived in part from the case of a professional athlete who fathered a child out of wedlock. In effect, if your income is high enough that the child support formula produces a child support payment higher than your children's needs (which can be hard to prove), the court can limit child support to your children's needs, or implement other measures, such as appointing a professional financial guardian, to make sure that your children (and not your spouse) realize the benefits of the child support payments. Typically, this will only be applicable if your earnings are several million dollars a year and your spouse has minimal income, including investment income, after leaving the divorce. This is rarely the case because in this factual scenario, your spouse would probably have income, at least partially consisting of alimony, which is part of the child support calculation.

Also, in some instances, it is possible that a parent can be ordered to pay additional expenses of the children over and above the child support amount. These expenses can include private school, camps, and other expenses that add up quickly. However, a parent can only be ordered to pay these expenses in addition to child support, if there is a long track record of doing so during the marriage, the parent has the financial ability to continue paying the expenses after the divorce, and the best interests of the children require the expenses to be paid.

In case you were wondering, most jurisdictions have laws stating child support is a "right of the child" and cannot be avoided, meaning that under the law, parents cannot simply agree there will be no child support, unless the facts of their situation yield a child support calculation of zero using the applicable child support formula.

In our experience, some judges here in Florida will approve agreements stating no child support will be paid by either parent, if the child support formula yields a result close to zero and it is obvious that one parent is not being intimidated into not having enough money to take care of the children, and has enough money to avoid using public benefits as a result.

In Florida and many other jurisdictions, child support is payable until the child is 18 years old, or until they graduate high school, if they are still in school on their 18th birthday. A few jurisdictions have laws requiring child support into adulthood, but that is an exception and not the norm. The practical meaning of this is that you are legally required to pay for your child until they reach high school graduation age, and cannot be legally obligated under most laws to pay for their college education.

Typically, child support can be changed whenever there is a significant change in the income of the person paying or receiving child support, as long as it does not appear the change in income comes from a deliberate strategy to avoid child support. Also, as with alimony, non-payment of child support without a valid excuse can cause serious problems, including cancellation of driver's licenses and passports, and even incarceration.

The Basics of Attorney's Fee & Cost Sharing Laws

In the United States, one of the underpinnings of the legal system is that in most forms of litigation, each person is responsible for paying their own attorney unless a judge determines the lawsuit was frivolous. This concept gave rise to "contingency fee lawyers." These lawyers are only paid a percentage of the money they recover for their client, which in effect allows these lawyers (some of which are extraordinary) to represent people who would otherwise lack the financial means to pay a lawyer.

Unfortunately, when it comes to divorce, many jurisdictions prohibit lawyers from working on a contingent fee basis, which results in the issue of each spouse needing to have the ability to pay the lawyer representing them in their divorce. At first blush, this is a problem for spouses who do not control enough of the marital financial resources to pay a competent divorce lawyer.

Many jurisdictions, including Florida where we practice, addressed this issue by enacting attorney's fee and litigation cost sharing laws. These laws are, in theory, developed and implemented to allow both spouses to be on equal legal footing in their divorce. The thought is that the government has an interest in making sure people are treated fairly in their divorce, because if one spouse is railroaded and becomes financially destitute, they could become a welfare recipient that eats up tax dollars which could be better spent elsewhere. Most state governments determined that having laws designed to encourage equal access to attorneys in a divorce, helps make it less likely that people will be taken advantage of in divorce negotiations.

Generally speaking, the attorney's fee and cost sharing laws operate to require a spouse with an obviously "superior" financial position after the divorce, to be responsible for all or a portion of their spouse's "reasonable" attorney's fees and costs. If both people leave the marriage with comparable net assets and income, they will likely be required to pay for their own lawyer.

These laws only apply if one spouse has a clearly "superior" financial position, which is usually interpreted to mean that (1) they leave the marriage with a substantially higher net worth or (2) they have the ability to pay their spouse's legal fees out of their net income after the divorce after taking into account any alimony or child support obligations and being able to pay their own reasonable living expenses. There are exceptions to these fee and cost sharing laws that limit the responsibility for paying legal fees when the spouse with "less money" leaves the marriage with still significant assets or engages in unnecessary litigation.

A notable issue when it comes to legal fees is a judge can order them to be paid "temporarily" by one spouse early on, with a final adjustment at the end of the divorce to create any inequalities. Spouses who do not have any meaningful access to cash or credit can seek to have their attorney paid through a "temporary" attorney fee request, which can be set by a judge but is sometimes negotiated between the lawyers so that spouses do not end up paying their divorce lawyers to fight in court about how much money is paid to divorce lawyers.

Although the theory behind the attorney fee and cost sharing laws seems admirable, the fact that one spouse can be responsible for all or a part of their (angry) spouse's legal expenses, can enable protracted divorce litigation in a situation when one person is likely to end up paying another person's legal fees. This is especially true when the angry spouse is not a sophisticated consumer of legal services and/or they blindly trust their lawyer due to a lack of trust in the relationship.

This means you need to have a *Best Divorce Strategy* aimed at resolving your divorce through negotiation or judicial intervention as soon as possible. The longer the divorce drags on, the more time your spouse's attorney has to generate the legal fees you could end up paying.

The analysis of whether someone has to pay their spouse's lawyer is fact intensive, and will vary between judges and jurisdictions. Your divorce lawyer will be able to give you a better feel for how your judge will address the issue. However, for illustration purposes, we have included several examples below modeled after how attorney's fee and cost sharing laws work where we practice law in Florida.

Scenario #1: Jack and Jill get divorced after 30 years of marriage and four children. Jack runs a small, but successful contracting business while Jill has primarily been a stay-at-home housewife once their children were born. In the divorce, both Jack and Jill leave the marriage with $350,000 in net marital assets, and Jack pays child support and alimony that allows Jill to meet her financial needs, but nothing more. Jack, after paying alimony, child support, and his own modest living expenses, has almost zero cash flow left over at the end of the month. In this situation, it is likely that both Jack and Jill are going to have to pay their own legal fees in the divorce. This is because, when all is said and done, Jack and Jill have the same amount of assets and neither has significant cash flow after paying for their basic living expenses.

Scenario #2: Assume the same facts in scenario #1 above, except Jack is an investment banker and has an additional $500,000 net cash flow each year, after paying alimony and child support to Jill. In this situation, although Jack and Jill are leaving the marriage with equal assets, Jack will likely pay most of Jill's legal fees and costs, since he can do so out of his net income. The same result would likely apply if Jack had no significant net cash flow after paying support expenses and his own living expenses as in scenario #1, but left the marriage with non-marital assets that he could utilize to pay Jill's lawyer.

Scenario #3: Assume the same facts as scenario #1, except that Jack and Jill both leave the marriage with net assets equal to $5 million. In this scenario, Jack and Jill would likely be required to pay for their own divorce lawyer. If the facts changed to where Jack left the marriage with $10 million and Jill receives $5 million, only one-half of Jack's net worth, the result would likely still be that each spouse would pay their own lawyer, as the fee and cost sharing laws are usually not going to apply when once each spouse has significant assets.

Scenario #4: Assume that Jack was a womanizer and Jill got fed up with Jack's philandering ways during their engagement and called off the wedding. Fast forward to 30 years later. Jack has been the serial bachelor, having never married, but having long enjoyed the affluent lifestyle created by his software business. However, at age 55 he is finally ready to settle down with the much younger, but seemingly sophisticated Jane. Jack and Jane tie the knot, but after the new couple returns from the wedding in Tahiti that Jack paid for (along with the airfare and accommodations for 75 of Jane's closest friends and family members) things start to go down-hill quickly. After less than one year of marriage, Jane files for divorce, at a time when Jack has liquid assets of $25 million, all of which are non-marital and will be kept by Jack in the divorce. Jane needs help paying her lawyer, because the only thing she has to her name is student loan debt from the college degree she stopped pursuing once she met Jack.

In this situation, Jack will likely pay for Jane's lawyer since he has significantly more money. However, if it is proven that Jane is engaging in frivolous divorce litigation as a means to extort money from Jack which she would never receive under the applicable law, the judge in her case will be more likely to make her pay her own lawyer, or at least limit Jack's legal fee and cost sharing exposure to what normal legal fees should have been, had Jane acted in good faith during the divorce.

The Basics of Enforcing & Challenging Prenuptial Agreements

Many people believe that if they signed a prenuptial agreement before getting married, then that agreement automatically governs their divorce. Unfortunately for some, and fortunately for others, the mere fact that a prenuptial agreement was signed does not mean the judge in your case will require it to be followed. In some cases, it is possible for you or your spouse to convince a judge to invalidate the agreement, meaning that your divorce will proceed as if the prenuptial agreement never existed.

The issue of whether a judge can set aside/invalidate a prenuptial agreement can be the difference between one spouse leaving the marriage with nothing or with millions of dollars. For this reason, disputes over the validity of prenuptial agreements are much more likely to be litigated and taken to trial than most other issues that arise in a divorce.

In deciding this litigation, Florida and many other jurisdictions operate under some version of the Uniform Premarital Agreement Act. Under this law, a prenuptial agreement will not be enforced if any of the following scenarios are proven: (1) either spouse did not voluntarily sign the agreement; (2) the agreement was the "product" of fraud, duress, coercion, or overreaching; or (3) the agreement was "unconscionable" when signed, and before the agreement was signed, there was not an adequate exchange of financial disclosure, an intelligent waiver of financial disclosure, or reasonable knowledge of the other spouse's finances.

If a prenuptial agreement was signed before 2007, a different framework applies in Florida that makes it slightly easier to invalidate a prenuptial agreement. Also, some jurisdictions will not recognize a prenuptial agreement if the conduct of the spouses during the marriage indicates the spouses chose to abandon the agreement.

The issue of whether a prenuptial agreement is enforced or invalidated requires an extremely fact intensive analysis. The main issues typically explored in this analysis are discussed in greater detail below, and include: (1) did both spouses have lawyers or access to lawyers; (2) did each spouse have the legal "capacity to contract" without "external pressures" putting either spouse in unequal bargaining positions; and (3) did each spouse have a solid understanding of the other spouse's finances to allow them to

reasonably evaluate the terms of the agreement.

Access to lawyers:

It is easier to convince a divorce court judge to invalidate (not recognize) a prenuptial agreement if it is shown that one spouse did not have a lawyer or the ability to access a lawyer to help them review the agreement. In other words, if a prenuptial agreement prepared by your lawyer was given to your spouse in a situation where they did not have any real ability to find legal counsel, it is probably going to be easier for your spouse to argue that circumstances of the agreement were unfair, and the agreement should be invalidated. However, the fact that you or your spouse did not have a lawyer does not, by itself, mean the prenuptial agreement will be invalidated. If it is proven that a spouse could have hired a lawyer but chose not to do so, then the "I didn't have a lawyer defense" will probably fail.

Capacity to Contract & External Pressures:

Prenuptial agreements are usually invalidated when one party is shown to have lacked the legal capacity to contract. As an example, if a spouse was intoxicated or shown to be temporarily insane when they signed the agreement, the intoxication or insanity should serve as a valid defense to the prenuptial agreement contract.

The "external pressures" defense is essentially a sub-set of the "incapacity to contract defense." The legal verbiage sometimes used to describe the "external pressures defense" includes "duress", "coercion", "overreaching", and "undue influence." Except in cases where a spouse literally had a gun to their head when they were given the prenuptial agreement (which we have yet to see), this defense comes up most commonly when a prenuptial agreement is signed close to a wedding. If an agreement is given to a spouse the day of the wedding, or very close to a wedding, it is possible to successfully argue that the spouse was under "duress" and other "external pressures" and thus, lacked the capacity to contract.

Whether a prenuptial agreement can be invalidated for being signed close to a wedding requires a thorough analysis of the history of the negotiations, relative competency of each spouse, and fairness of the contract. The fact that a prenuptial agreement was signed close to a wedding is not dispositive. A relatively fair agreement that was negotiated over several months, and signed close to the wedding between two legally sophisticated spouses, is much more likely to be enforced than an agreement that was first discussed on the wedding day, where one spouse was not legally sophisticated and lacked knowledge of the other spouse's finances when signing the agreement.

A hurdle to the "incapacity to contract" or "external pressures" defenses to prenuptial agreements is showing the agreement was not "ratified" during the marriage. "Ratification" occurs when people take affirmative action to reaffirm their commitment to a contract they might otherwise have invalidated due to an "incapacity to contract defense," "external pressures defense," or another legal defense to a contract. When a prenuptial agreement has been ratified, the agreement usually cannot be invalidated under the "incapacity to contract" or "external pressures" doctrines.

The determination of whether a prenuptial agreement has been ratified usually comes down to determining whether the party seeking to invalidate the agreement accepted any material benefits due to them under the agreement that they would not otherwise be obligated to receive in absence of the agreement.

As an example, if a wife was due a high monthly spending allowance under a prenuptial agreement, and after signing the agreement and getting married, accepted the monthly spending allowance each month during the marriage, it is likely to be determined that the wife "ratified" the prenuptial agreement by her conduct of accepting the high monthly spending allowance. If this was the case, the wife in this example would probably not be allowed to argue the "incapacity to contract defense" in her divorce. The theory behind this is that, the wife, though she lacked the capacity to contract, should have tried to get out of the contract, instead of following it for the entire marriage.

Disclosure of Finances:

If a prenuptial agreement was signed after 2007 in Florida or other states following the Uniform Premarital Agreement Act, then it is possible to waive all disclosure of finances in connection with a prenuptial agreement. However, if the agreement was not signed before 2007, or did not explicitly state that financial disclosure was waived, then the agreement can be set aside if there was no reasonable exchange of financial disclosure between both parties. For a spouse to set aside an agreement on account of a lack of financial disclosure, they usually must prove both that (1) the terms of the agreement were "unconscionable" and (2) that they did not have a reasonable idea of their spouse's finances at the time they

signed the agreement.

In other words, in most cases, courts will not set aside a fair prenuptial agreement on account of there being a lack of financial disclosure. Also, a spouse cannot seek to invalidate a prenuptial agreement based on insufficient financial disclosure, if it is proven they had a clear understanding of the details of their spouse's finances when the agreement was negotiated.

Although some of the law relating to prenuptial agreements and whether they can be enforced or set aside, appears to be "common sense," remember that only the basics of the law are covered here. As the saying goes, "the devil is in the details." The bottom line is that, if there is a prenuptial agreement at play, you will need to thoroughly review the facts and circumstances of the negotiation and terms of the agreement with your divorce lawyer, to determine whether the agreement is likely to be enforced.

The Basics of Several Other Legal Issues

At this point, your education about the basics of the laws that will apply to the dissolution of your marriage is almost complete. Your knowledge of concepts explained in this chapter will allow you to "know what you need to know" about the law, to continue towards the process of preparing for divorce and meeting with a qualified divorce lawyer. If you have not done so already, we encourage you to make a list of all of your questions about how the law might apply to your situation, so that you can go over those questions when you meet with an attorney later in the process.

Until that time, we've included short explanations of several other legal issues that sometimes will relate to divorce.

"No Fault" Grounds for Divorce:

There is a misconception among many people we meet that obtaining a divorce requires proof of "fault," such as adultery, abandonment, or cruelty. This was true several decades ago, but as of 2010, every state in the United States of America allows "no fault divorce." In most jurisdictions, all that needs to happen to obtain a divorce is one spouse alleging that there are "irreconcilable differences" in the marriage. In other words, if you want to get a divorce, you can get a divorce, and there is really nothing your spouse can do to stop the process.

Incapacity to Get Divorced:

The exception to the "no fault" automatic divorce in some jurisdictions, including in Florida where we practice, is that if one spouse is legally incapacitated (such as in a coma or found to be legally incompetent) the divorce can be delayed for three years. Although we have seen nefarious spouses pretend to be legally insane to invoke this exception to the no-fault divorce law for bargaining purposes, this rarely ever happens. As a practical matter, the three year "incapacity waiting period" is rarely a real problem because in most instances people will be focused on initially caring for their spouse and not divorcing them, and the risks relating to incurring liabilities for medical care can be hedged by filing a divorce petition or postnuptial agreement.

Spousal Spying/Recording:

In the age of the "internet of everything," it seems like almost all of what we do leaves an electronic footprint somewhere. As a result, the actions of ourselves and our family are even easier to track, especially with the advent of services like the "iCloud," which allows emails and text messages (once the secret conduit of affairs) to show up on multiple devices (including that old iPad you forgot about, and allowed your spouse to use). Further, with the use of spyware and recording programs, the amount of information that can be obtained is almost limitless.

In most instances, courts consider information on shared devices or accounts to be "fair game" to accumulation by both people in a divorce. Further, there is usually not going to be a problem if you use a shared password or standard password to access and gather electronic information. The theory is that the sharing of an account or password equates to your spouse's consent to you having the information.

Many courts look at electronic accounts with shared passwords as the digital equivalent of an unlocked physical file cabinet sitting in the marital home. There is no law against going into and copying paper files in that unlocked file cabinet in your home office. So, why would it be a problem to access a shared electronic file? Although the laws can vary between jurisdictions, obtaining digital information usually only becomes a problem if passwords, information, or access was obtained using illegal spyware programs.

As it relates to recording, to be safe, it is illegal in most jurisdictions to record phone calls or conversations in private places without notice to the other party (this is why most customer service phone numbers state up front that the call "may" be recorded) or the recording is not obvious. However, conversations can be recorded in public places where there would be no expectation of privacy. Furthermore, video recording (without audio) can be done in most circumstances without notice.

As it relates to vehicle tracking, most jurisdictions allow you to have GPS monitoring devices on a vehicle, if you are on the title to that vehicle. This means, you could get in trouble for putting a tracking device on your spouse's car, if your name is not on the title. That said, it is very difficult to prove who implanted a tracking device, and the utility of such devices are starting to become obsolete, now that most phones can be tracked through shared account settings.

Domestic Violence & Restraining Orders:

If your spouse abuses you physically or threatens to harm you, then you should call the police immediately and seek protection from every available option in your jurisdiction. In most jurisdictions, there is a process to obtain a restraining order (sometimes called an injunction) if your spouse has physically harmed you or created a reasonable fear of imminent harm to you. Once one of these orders is issued, your spouse is usually required to stay away from you and cease all communication with you. The courts take violation of restraining orders/injunctions very seriously. Usually, someone will be jailed for violating the terms of a restraining order/injunction.

Freezing Bank Accounts:

In some instances, when a marital estate is concentrated in one or two bank accounts, there is a legitimate fear that a spouse will "take the money and run" or otherwise transfer the money to unknown accounts, thereby making the divorce a game of "find the money" or at least more complicated than necessary. If this is the case, most jurisdictions provide a process for temporarily "freezing" an account. Sometimes, this can be done without a court order and merely by a notice from your lawyer (called a "lis pendens") to a financial institution, stating that an account is being claimed by you as part of a divorce case. Most banks, at least initially, err on the side of caution, and will freeze major transactions in an account upon receiving such a notice, out of fear of being sued later.

Learn What Is Important About the Divorce Court Process & Timing

Why You Need to Know About the Legal Process

The development of your *Best Divorce* strategy cannot take place in a vacuum. For your *Best Divorce* strategy to be realistic and effective, it must be designed after taking into account the procedural stages of your divorce once it starts in the court system, and the timing of those stages. Although your *Best Divorce* strategy may be designed to avoid litigation, it is important at this point to have a general idea of what will likely happen through the court system, if your case is not resolved quickly.

And on the issue of divorce strategy, you should consider reading Control Your Difficult Divorce, the Bruce Law Firm's divorce strategy guide. The book is available for free download at www.ControlYourDifficultDivorce.com.

Anyway, entire books have been written about the process and procedure of divorce litigation. Those books are useful to the lawyers, but can be overwhelming and confusing to everyone else. Frankly, there is no need for you to memorize or even try to understand the rules of procedure. To save you this unnecessary "pleasure," we've summarized "what you need to know" about the primary stages of divorce litigation in the remainder of this section. As with learning the basics of the law in the first section of this book, you should take note of anything about divorce procedures that leaves you wanting to "know more" or you think could be particularly relevant in your divorce, and then make sure to get your questions answered later when you consult with an attorney (more information on lawyers is available in the Bruce Law Firm's book, How to Find, Hire, & Work With Your Divorce Lawyer, which is available for free download at www.AllAboutDivorceLawyers.com).

The Divorce Lawsuit Filing & Responses

Divorce cases are formally started in Florida and in most other jurisdictions, by filing a Divorce Petition with the appropriate court. Technically speaking, the Divorce Petition is a "lawsuit," meaning that to get divorced you have to "sue" your spouse through the state court system. It's worth noting that either you or your spouse must have been living in Florida for at least six months prior to filing the divorce lawsuit. If the lawsuit is filed too early, then the court will deny the divorce. If you have lived in Florida less than six months, you either need to "wait it out" or consider filing for divorce back where you used to live. The same type of "waiting period" laws apply in most other jurisdictions, some often counties, that promote "fly in" divorces (that unfortunately don't usually hold up elsewhere).

The general rule is that divorce lawsuits will usually be filed in the county where you and your spouse last resided as a couple. The main exception to this rule is that if children have lived in another state for at least six months, the issues related to the children will have to be dealt with in the state where the children are located. In this instance, the other issues, besides the children (dividing property, spousal support, etc.), will be determined by the court in the state where you and your spouse last lived as a married couple.

As to the Divorce Petition itself, the basic purpose of the document is to put your spouse on formal notice that (1) you are seeking a legal dissolution of your marriage and (2) of "what you want" in the divorce (such as whether you are seeking alimony, attorney's fees, or any special restrictions related to your children). In most cases, a Divorce Petition is not a very impressive document. Although you could probably write several books about your marriage and why it is ending, the Divorce Petition will not contain any of that information. In most cases, what is written in the Divorce Petition will be limited only to what is necessary to allow a divorce court judge to give you "what you want" in the rare instance that your divorce must be resolved through a trial.

After the Divorce Petition is filed with the court, it must be "served" on your spouse, just like any other lawsuit. The Divorce Petition can be "served" by a process server, surprising your spouse at their office, when they are engaged in "extracurricular activities" with someone else, and in several other interesting scenarios. In some instances, your *Best Divorce* strategy may include this type of "service by shock and surprise." That said, usually this type of tactic is not necessary. In many instances, the Divorce Petition will be "served" by email, with your spouse or their attorney signing a document that eliminates the need to have a process server formally "serve" your spouse.

Once the Divorce Petition is filed and served, several different deadlines become triggered that assist your divorce with staying on track for a resolution. First, your spouse will have twenty days after being served to file their response to your Divorce Petition. Second, a forty-five-day deadline starts for producing what is called "Mandatory Disclosure," which usually consists of three years of tax returns, three months of bank and credit card statements, and several other items constituting the "bare necessitates" of financial disclosure. We note a separate chapter on financial disclosure follows this chapter.

As to your spouse's response to your Divorce Petition, they will file a document with the court called an "Answer" that admits or denies the allegations made in your Divorce Petition. This will include their basic position on whether or not you are entitled to what you requested in the Divorce Petition, as to things like alimony, division of property, restrictions on parenting issues, and attorney's fees. Also, it is more likely than not that your spouse will file their own Divorce Petition, called a "Counter-Petition" that lays out "what they want" from you in the divorce. You, in turn, will then file your "Answer" to the "Counter-Petition" in the same manner your spouse did to your "Divorce Petition."

Normally, it takes about six to eight weeks for both you and your spouse to have filed all applicable "Divorce Petitions," "Counter-Petitions," and required "Answers" to these filings. At this point, the divorce court judge is considered to be on notice of all of the issues in your case, and the law allows the judge to set a trial date if you or your spouse requests a trial. Typically, the trial will not occur for at least several months, and will sometimes be over a year away depending on the judge. In the time before trial, you and your lawyer will work towards exchanging financial documents and attempting to settle your case. All of which is covered in the remainder of this section.

The Initial Exchange of Financial Records

Lawyers and judges have developed a term to describe the process of making you provide your spouse with what can seem like an endless pile of paper and information. Instead of calling the process an "intrusion", an "invasion" or an "information overload," the profession settles on calling the process, "Discovery." In all seriousness, this exchange of financial information can be one of the most important aspects of your divorce as it will allow you and your team to ensure you are getting a fair settlement and prepare your case for trial if your case does not settle.

The strategy we advocate is for you to gather as much financial information as possible prior to hiring a lawyer so that you are more informed about your financial situation. In fact, the Bruce Law Firm has a book devoted to this subject titled The Women's Guide to Getting Organized for Divorce, available for free download at www.GetOrganizedForDivorce.com. Although the book is tailored towards women considering divorce from a narcissistic or emotionally abusive/manipulative husband, it is useful to both men and women alike.

Anyway, in a perfect world, you would be able to get all of the financial information you needed to settle your divorce on fair terms through this process. However, even if you follow our preparation protocols, there may be (and usually is) a need for you and your lawyer to spend some time gathering information from your spouse and their banks and businesses. Even if you do not need to gather anymore information the odds are that your spouse or their lawyer will not be as organized or informed as you and there will be a need to spend time exchanging financial records. The name for this process is the "Discovery Process" (doesn't this sound fun!?).

Florida and many other jurisdictions have set some bare minimums on documents that spouses are supposed to exchange while negotiating a divorce settlement. The items included in the minimum disclosure are referred to as "Mandatory Disclosure" and include:

1. A Financial Affidavit, which is a document that discloses all of your income, expenses, assets and liabilities and is signed under oath;

2. Three years of tax returns;

3. Three months of statements for checking accounts and credit cards;

4. One year of statements for savings accounts, brokerage accounts, and tax deferred retirement accounts;

5. Copies of any deeds, leases, and titles;

6. Proof of insurance coverage; and

7. Documentation showing whether any assets are non-marital.

It is possible for informed spouses to waive the exchange of "Mandatory Disclosure." However, in practice, the "Mandatory Disclosure" documents are usually "only the beginning" of the financial information requested and exchanged between attorneys in a divorce case. In practice, it is common for most lawyers to file a request for three years of all bank and credit card statements, including copies of cancelled checks. Further, when there is a business involved, most competent lawyers are going to request three years of balance sheets and profit and loss statements, at least a year's worth of records relating to the general ledger of the business, and copies of the corporate records, including bylaws, partnership agreements, and stock certificates.

In addition to seeking records from your spouse, it is also possible to seek information from other people, business and banks, through the subpoena power of your lawyer. Although there are some restrictions and costs involved, it's usually possible to directly request these sources of potential information to "tell you what they know" and give you copies of any records in their possession. This can be especially helpful when your spouse has a personal or business accountant, or an involved financial advisor or attorney. Instead of waiting around for your spouse to give you records, you can use a subpoena to obtain the information directly from these other people who are usually unlikely to risk their professional livelihood by tampering with documents.

In many instances, you will be able to develop a thorough understanding of your spouse's income, and the assets and liabilities that will need to be split up, after an initial exchange of financial discovery and potentially the receipt of information subpoenaed through other people, banks, or businesses. At this point, if you have not yet negotiated a settlement, your lawyer will likely suggest that you attend mediation, which is covered in the next chapter of this book. However, if you or your lawyer still "need some questions answered," it might be necessary to first take your spouse's deposition before mediation. The topic of depositions is also explained later in this section.

Settling Your Divorce Through Mediation

Fortunately, the majority of divorce cases are resolved between spouses and lawyers before a divorce court judge makes any major decisions. One of the most common ways for such a resolution is through a process called Mediation, which usually occurs soon after spouses exchange financial information. This is usually two to three months after a divorce case is filed, but can be earlier, and even before the lawsuit is filed, if both spouses are motivated to settle and have a solid understanding of the marital finances.

The Mediation itself is an informal out of court meeting that will usually take place at the office of one of the spouse's lawyers or at the Mediator's office. Typically, each spouse will be in a separate office or conference room with their lawyer, and a person called the "Mediator" will go between each room to learn each spouse's settlement positions, and then help facilitate the negotiation of a final settlement of all or some of the issues involved with the divorce.

What is said, offered, or done in Mediation is nearly always confidential. This usually means that nobody can be required to testify in court about what settlement offers were made, or what facts were discussed in Mediation. The idea behind keeping Mediation confidential is to create an environment where spouses are encouraged to negotiate and freely discuss issues in order to facilitate a settlement.

In many instances, if spouses reach an agreement as to the settlement terms at the Mediation, a formal settlement offer will be prepared on the spot for each spouse to review and sign before leaving the Mediation. Many of the best lawyers will go to the Mediation with a draft settlement agreement already prepared reflecting their client's desired settlement to allow the document to be quickly signed when an agreement is reached.

Most successful Mediations will take two to six hours to complete, although it is not unheard of for Mediations to take all day long or expand into multiple days when the case calls for the resolution of complex issues. That said, a Mediation can be done almost immediately after it begins, if neither spouse is agreeable to settling any issue. This is because there is no requirement for spouses to do anything more during Mediation, besides showing up, and at least briefly, attempting to negotiate in good faith.

Nobody can be forced to do anything else at Mediation. If you do not want to settle based on the offers discussed at Mediation, you do not have to settle.

Most of the best Mediators are divorce lawyers themselves, or are least are familiar with divorce laws, the divorce process, and the divorce judge who has been assigned to the case. Typically, Mediators charge by the hour, and fees commonly paid for Mediators in South Florida where I practice will range between $175-500 per hour. It is customary for the spouses to split the payment of the Mediator's fee, but this can be negotiated, and if there is a major income disparity, the spouse with the higher income will usually foot the bill.

Although the cost of paying a lawyer and at least half of the Mediator's fee can seem expensive, Mediation is usually the most efficient way to resolve a case quickly. In most instances, the negotiation of settlement agreement terms between two busy lawyers (who have to get their client's approval before submitting each subsequent draft of a settlement agreement) can take weeks or months to complete, and ends up costing more money than it would to just "sit down and knock things out" at a Mediation.

Mediation works; plain and simple. Judges know this too. As a result, many divorce court judges and local courts have adopted rules that spouses are required to attend at least one Mediation session before scheduling a court hearing on major issues. Many judges think that if families are forced to go to Mediation they may not have a need to pay lawyers to go to court. This philosophy makes sense, but the "no Mediation, no court hearing" rule sometimes prompts people with bad intentions to either (1) delay Mediation to keep someone from getting a court hearing or (2) to force Mediation before enough information has been exchanged to have productive and informed settlement negotiations for purposes of trying to speed up getting into court.

Our view is that, barring emergencies, Mediation should happen as soon as possible. But only after spouses have exchanged the information that allows them to negotiate in good faith and with an understanding of the marital finances to at least allow the lawyers to have a reasonable degree of certainty as to how a judge might decide the case. This is because a *Best Divorce* settlement offer will need to take into account the potential outcome in court along with other variables.

Also, it should go without saying that you should plan to meet with your attorney well in advance of the Mediation to discuss what type of settlement makes sense, and to get a meeting of the minds with your lawyer on what your bottom line, acceptable settlement represents. This will allow the lawyer to plan and implement a mediation strategy designed to obtain your desired result.

Some people confuse Mediation with Arbitration. Arbitration is considered a form of "alternative dispute resolution" that allows people to avoid the court system. However, Arbitration vastly differs from Mediation as it is essentially nothing more than a trial in front of a private judge, or a panel of private judges, who then issue a binding decision that, unlike judge or jury decisions, can rarely be appealed. Arbitration does not involve any negotiations, and unlike Mediation, involves decisions being made by professional arbitrators (these are basically private judges) instead of the spouses. Although some people elect to use Arbitration to speed up the resolution of their case, the use of Arbitration in family court proceedings is rare and usually cannot be used to decide child custody issues.

Mediation is also compared with a process called "Collaborative Divorce," which is a separate subject covered in the next chapter.

A Word About Collaborative Law/Divorce

Mediation is similar, but not the same, as a process called "Collaborative Law" or "Collaborative Divorce." In a nutshell, Collaborative Divorce involves a process where each party hires an attorney to help them negotiate a settlement, usually before any lawsuit is filed, with the understanding that each person will need to get a new attorney if the negotiations fail and litigation is necessary. Further, usually an accountant and mental health professional will be jointly hired to work with both spouses and their lawyer as part of the process.

Collaborative Divorce can be effective, but our personal belief is that it usually is appropriate only when each side has equal access to information, nobody is concerned about the amount of time needed to resolve the divorce, and the marital finances will not be significantly depleted through extended negotiations. Our belief is that most of the families that meet these rare criteria are also prime candidates for resolving their divorces quickly through an early Mediation, which still allows for an amicable and dignified divorce while allowing each spouse to (1) obtain a court hearing or trial much quicker if negotiations fail while (2) avoiding the Collaborative Divorce requirement of each spouse having to "start all over again" with a new lawyer if the case cannot be settled. Further, in many instances, starting with a Collaborative Divorce will blow most of the basic elements of leverage and strategy designed to obtain a fair resolution as efficiently and as quickly as possible.

We believe most of the spouses who push for Collaborative Divorce are either (1) doing so with the ulterior motive of keeping their spouse from digging deeper into their finances or (2) are uneducated as to the benefits and likelihood of success of settling a case through mediation. We believe many nefarious spouses propose Collaborative Divorce to manufacture a situation where their spouse feels compelled to settle based on a lack of information, due to the "sunk costs" of paying the Collaborative Divorce lawyer, and the knowledge that they will have to pay even more money to educate a new lawyer and wait potentially a year or more to get a trial date if negotiations fail. Our philosophy is: Why take on these risks when you can settle your case quickly and amicably through a traditional divorce mediation?

If what you desire is some sort of romantic/eclectic negotiating experience with your spouse outside of litigation, we think you should skip Collaborative Divorce and go to marriage counseling instead. You will still get to attend regular sit-down sessions with your spouse to negotiate terms related to your marriage, except you don't have to pay any lawyers. The entire process can be covered by insurance, and you don't have to get divorced!

Okay, we might be biased against Collaborative Divorce, and think it is a waste of time and money and is nothing more than a marketing scheme designed by the accountants, financial planners, and mental health professionals who are involved in the "collaborative" process to manufacture demand for their services, but… the process is one of the available options to utilize in your divorce and information is readily available about it online, so if you are interested, type "Collaborative Divorce" into your favorite search engine and you will be able to learn more about the process, which you can then discuss with the lawyers you interview.

The Uncontested Final Hearing & Final Judgment

Many people will be able to reach an agreement with their spouse at some point between exchanging financial information and attending Mediation. When this happens, one of the spouses will go with their attorney to attend what is sometimes referred to as an "Uncontested Final Hearing" in order to finalize the divorce and obtain the "Final Judgment" that legally dissolves the marriage.

The Uncontested Final Hearing is a relatively straightforward court hearing that usually lasts less than five minutes. Typically, only one spouse is required to attend the hearing with their lawyer. During the hearing, the divorce court judge will review the settlement agreement and will question the spouse to make sure they actually want to be divorced, understand the settlement agreement, and were not forced into the agreement against their will. If there are children, the divorce court judge will also review certain aspects of the settlement agreement to make sure that it contains adequate provisions for child support and at least gives a basic explanation of each parent's rights and responsibilities over the children. In nearly all cases, as long as the settlement agreement needs the basic requirements of the law, the judge will accept and approve the agreement.

Otherwise, the only other thing that really happens at this hearing is the judge will require proof that the spouse in attendance was a resident of the jurisdiction long enough to allow the court to grant the divorce (usually you must live in the jurisdiction for six-months prior to filing for divorce for there to be jurisdiction). Usually establishing this proof does not involve anything more than showing the divorce court judge a copy of a driver's license with an issue date at least six months before the divorce case was filed.

As long as the residency requirements are established and the divorce court judge accepts the settlement agreement (which nearly always happens), the judge will conclude the Uncontested Final Hearing by signing the Final Judgment and granting the divorce.

As to the Final Judgment itself, it is nothing more than what is usually two or three pages of paper that is signed by the divorce court judge. Prior to the Uncontested Final Hearing, the lawyers for both spouses will prepare and agree to the wording of the Final Judgment and bring copies of the document to the

Uncontested Final Hearing for the divorce court judge to sign if he or she approves of the settlement agreement. The Final Judgment will almost always attach and incorporate the settlement agreement. As a result, the Final judgment effectively operates to require both spouses to follow all of the terms of the settlement agreement, and makes failure to follow the agreement equivalent to violating a court order.

For many people, the divorce court judge signing the Final Judgment at the Uncontested Final Hearing will be the end of the legal case involving their divorce. Hopefully, your divorce will be finalized through this process very early on before time, money, and relationships are burned.

The remainder of this section goes on to explain the temporary hearings, depositions, trials, and appeals that can take place when spouses do not reach a settlement agreement at or before mediation.

Temporary Relief Hearings

Given the amount of time it can take to finalize a divorce through the legal system, it is sometimes necessary for divorce court judges to make rulings early on in a case, to address issues relating to support, children, and other financial matters such as making one spouse contribute towards the payment of the other's legal fees and costs. The divorce court judges address these issues through what is called a "temporary relief hearing."

Temporary relief hearings are especially useful for "setting straight" the behavior of a spouse who cuts off their spouse/family financially, or plays wicked games with children for purposes of obtaining leverage in the early stages of the divorce. Divorce court judges understand that some spouses will go to extreme lengths to force their spouse into taking a poor settlement or dropping the divorce. When confronted with this type of behavior, the judge can issue orders to correct the situation by ordering payment of financial support, establishing a temporary custody schedule, and putting in place other temporary remedies like requiring one spouse to move out of the house, or pay for the other person's divorce lawyer.

Unless there is a life-or-death emergency, most divorce court judges will not allow spouses to schedule a temporary relief hearing until they have attempted to settle their divorce through a Mediation. The theory behind this is that since many people settle their entire divorce at an early mediation, everyone should try to do so before wasting public resources having the judge decide temporary issues that are only in effect until the divorce is finalized.

Temporary relief hearings are short. The hearing will usually only be thirty minutes in length, giving each spouse fifteen minutes to present their side of the case. This relatively brief amount of time is to present evidence from potentially multiple witnesses on issues that sometimes include both setting a temporary timesharing schedule for the children, determining alimony and child support, and addressing the issue of how much a spouse will need to pay their lawyer through trial.

The short amount of time allotted for these hearings makes it so only the important testimony and evidence is presented. Most people walk out of these hearings and wonder how the judge knows enough about their situation to decide anything. However, divorce court judges can regularly handle five or more of these types of hearings a week in addition to their regular trial schedule. As a result, after only a short time on the bench, divorce court judges essentially become machines programmed to hone in on the evidence they need to make temporary rulings.

The theory behind allotting such a brief amount of time for a hearing that can decide important financial and children's issues, is that sometimes people need a divorce court judge to "step in" and stabilize a family's situation by making a quick ruling that makes sure the basic bills continue to get paid, the children are okay, and that "status quo" is preserved as much as possible, while each spouse prepares their case for a final settlement or trial. The thought is that since the judge's decision is only "temporary", and any inequities can be corrected later, why allow spouses to take up hours of the court's time?

Although temporary relief rulings are supposed to be only temporary, the ruling can go a long way towards influencing a spouse to settle their case. In many instances, if the divorce court judge does not give a spouse what they want on a temporary alimony or child custody issue, the spouse will feel like they'll be fighting an uphill battle to get a different result from the same judge at trial.

Some people who are in this position end up settling their case

instead of paying their divorce lawyer the significant costs of trial to potentially get them the same result. With this being the case, if your spouse is making unreasonable settlement demands, your *Best Divorce* strategy might be to persuade your spouse to become more reasonable by getting the judge to take your side in a temporary relief hearing.

Depositions

A deposition is the process of an attorney asking a witness questions under oath. In the context of a divorce deposition, the witness will either be one of the spouses or another person who may know facts relevant to the issues in the divorce. Usually, the deposition will happen at a conference room table at the office of one of the lawyers or a court reporting company. The questions asked by the lawyers and answers given by the witness are recorded by a court reporter.

If you were to independently observe a deposition, all you would see is a several people sitting around a table, with one person being asked questions by a lawyer, and a court reporter sitting at the end of the table recording the questions asked and answers given by typing into a laptop or machine with a funny looking keyboard.

Each spouse's lawyer can ask questions of the witness at the deposition. In many cases, the court reporter will be asked to type out the recorded question and answer session between the lawyer and the witness at the deposition. The typed version of the deposition recording is called a "transcript." Transcripts are basically books, with the pages filled up with the lawyer's questions and the witnesses' answers typed out.

Both spouses are allowed to be at the deposition. This can occasionally make for an interesting situation. Just imagine being in the room as one spouse is watching on as the other spouse or their paramour explains the details of an adulterous affair. Some *Best Divorce* strategies involve scheduling depositions early on, or right after mediation, as some spouses would rather give up more in a settlement than go through the deposition experience (or at least think twice before turning down a reasonable offer if they know not settling means having to sit for their deposition).

That said, the primary purpose of depositions is to "pin down" the testimony of a spouse or other witness as it relates to each major issue in the divorce. This allows the lawyers to understand what makes up the basis for the spouse's position on the issues the divorce court judge will decide at trial. If a witnesses' testimony at trial is different than their deposition testimony, a good lawyer will exploit the difference to cast doubt upon whether the witness is telling the truth at trial.

Further, lawyers will use the depositions to assist them with advising their client on whether they should settle or take their case to trial. If the other spouse "presents well" by testifying in a convincing manner than a good attorney may counsel their client to think hard about settlement. On the same token, if the other spouse does not seem believable, or presents terrible justifications for their legal position, it may become easier to turn down an insulting settlement offer and proceed to trial.

Notably, in certain situations, the deposition transcript can be turned into evidence by being read to the judge at trial. From time to time, a spouse will give testimony in their deposition that supports the other spouse's case. When this happens, a seasoned trial lawyer can make for easy presentation of evidence by simply reading the other spouse's deposition transcript to the judge.

At the end of the day, while depositions are one of the most expensive aspects of litigation, they can be an extremely valuable tool for evaluating whether or not to settle a case, and are an "absolute must" when it comes to allowing your lawyer to prepare for trial.

Trial

If you and your spouse cannot settle all of the issues in your divorce, you can elect to have the issues still in controversy decided by a divorce court judge. Before the judge makes any decisions, each spouse has the opportunity to testify and present evidence to the judge in a final court hearing of the case, which can range in duration from several hours to several days. The name of this final hearing is commonly referred to as a "trial."

A trial in divorce court is not that much different than any other type of trial. The primary exception, however, is that with divorce court trials in most jurisdictions, all issues are determined by a judge. There is no jury.

A divorce trial starts like any other trial with each spouse's lawyer presenting opening statements. Notably, the spouse who filed for divorce first gets the "first say" in the opening statements. After opening statements, the presentation of witnesses and evidence begins. As with opening statements, the spouse who filed for divorce first gets the first opportunity to call all of their witnesses to testify and present their evidence, which is followed by the other spouse doing the same. In many divorce cases, the only witnesses will be each spouse and possibly a forensic accountant, although the more complicated cases or child custody cases can involve more witnesses. Depending on the jurisdiction and judge, each spouse may also get the opportunity to present rebuttal witnesses and rebuttal evidence.

Similar to jury trials, divorce court trials also end with closing arguments, with the spouse who was first to file for divorce getting to starting the closing arguments, and giving the final word in a rebuttal argument. However, unlike jury trials, there will rarely be any "verdict" announced at the end of trial. Instead, the divorce court judges will almost always issue a written ruling and explanation of their decisions on each contested issue. While many judges strive to release their written rulings quickly, it is not unheard of for some judges to take several months or even over a year to issue their written decision.

Given the delays and expenses inherent with having issues in your divorce determined by a divorce court judge after a full-blown trial, the *Best Divorce* strategies are often designed to avoid trial. Trials are usually appropriate only when the difference between a fair settlement and the other spouse's settlement position justifies the time and expense involved. Furthermore, there is a value to avoiding trials, as sometimes divorce court judges make honest mistakes or render unfair decisions. When this happens, it is necessary to continue paying lawyers to pursue a divorce court appeal, which is the subject of the next section.

Divorce Court Appeals

If you do not agree with the divorce court judge's ruling, it is possible to appeal the decision to have it reviewed by an appeals court. We could write an entire book about everything that is involved with appeals, and essentially did through the material that is published on our website www.DivorceCourtAppeals.com. For now, though, there is no advantage to having an extremely detailed understanding of the divorce court appeals process. The main thing to know at this point is how divorce court appeals differ from everything else that happens through trial in a divorce case.

The primary difference between divorce court appeals and divorce court litigation, is that nearly everything in an appeal happens on paper and behind closed doors. In an appeal, your position is presented to the appellate court through an "argument on paper," which is called an "appellate brief." In other words, in an appeal, there are no depositions and there is no trial where a judge will listen to testimony from each party. In most Florida divorce and child custody appeals, the entire case takes place on paper, with the lawyers explaining each spouse's position in the appellate briefs.

In some appeals there is a short hearing called an oral argument hearing. However, unlike a trial, an oral argument hearing is typically only twenty to forty minutes long, and consists only of legal argument from the attorneys to the appellate court judges. To be clear, there is no testimony from witnesses at an oral argument hearing- only legal arguments from each party's attorney. It must be noted that in most appellate courts it is rare for there to even be an oral argument hearing in a divorce appeal. Nearly all of such appeals are decided by the appellate court reading each party's legal briefs and making a written decision.

Another difference between appellate court and trial court litigation is the number of judges involved. With most appeals, there is typically going to be three judges that review and decide your case. In some instances, the three judges reviewing your case will initiate a process called "en banc review" that results in all of the judges at your appeals court (sometimes this is ten or more judges) taking part in deciding your case.

It should be noted that each appeals court judge employs several attorneys called law clerks. Law clerks are often from the top of the class at their law schools and play an integral part in the review of your case. Although the process varies from judge to judge, in many instances, the judges will have the law clerks review the appellate briefs and prepare what is called a "bench memorandum." This is a document that analyzes the legal arguments made by each spouse, usually with a recommendation as to which spouse is correct. The appeals court judge will then review the briefs and the law clerk's memorandum, before meeting with the other judges assigned to the case.

When the judges meet, there is a discussion of how whether each judge agrees or disagrees with the trial court's ruling. Ultimately, the decision to affirm or reverse the trial court's ruling is made by a majority vote between the judges. After a decision is reached, one of the judges will write the appellate court's decision, called an "opinion."

The amount of time that it takes for your appeal to finish will vary depending on the complexity of the issues presented, number of extensions granted to the attorneys, and whether or not the appellate court deems it necessary to expedite your appeal. Generally, most appeals take between six to eighteen months to conclude. However, when an appeal is expedited, the appeal can

be   over   in   as   little   as   several   weeks.

Our Other Books Designed to Help You

Hopefully you have found this book helpful to you in your time of need. In case you were looking to learn more, we wanted to make sure you knew that this is not the Bruce Law Firm's only book.

The Bruce Law Firm has several books available for free download at www.DivorceInformationBooks.com. These books are free and include this Florida Divorce Law Guide, the Women's Guide to Getting Organized for Divorce, How to Divorce Your Controlling, Manipulative, Narcissistic Husband, our guide on How to Find, Hire, & Work With Your Divorce Lawyer, and Control Your Difficult Divorce, our comprehensive divorce strategy guide.

Also, because it is our belief that the real best divorce is the divorce that didn't have to happen, the Bruce Law Firm developed and supports www.StayMarriedFlorida.com, a website devoted to helping couples build, have, and keep healthy relationships. The website has articles, podcast interviews, and a growing directory of extremely talented results-driven therapists.

If you found this free book helpful, the best compliment you could give would be to share our books with others who might be in need (just direct them to www.DivorceInformationBooks.com). Also, we love it when people spread the word about the Bruce Law Firm on Avvo.com (google Christopher R. Bruce Avvo or Ashley D. Bruce Avvo and click to leave a review) or our google business page (google Bruce Law Firm West Palm Beach and click the link to leave a google review).

ABOUT THE AUTHORS

 **Ashley D. Bruce is** a divorce lawyer in West Palm Beach and Wellington, Florida. She got her start in divorce_ from her mother, Bernice Alden Dillman, who practiced divorce and family law for over thirty years in Boca Raton. Growing up, Ashley often witnessed clients walk into her mother's office on the first day, distraught, insecure, and upset, and watched them blossom into being more confident, secure, and their knowing that a better life was ahead. Watching her mom guide clients through this transformation helped Ashley realize that she, too, wanted to help clients grow and have a better life.

Ashley's early experience shadowing her mother and handling complex business litigation and bankruptcy law (she did a lot of "bet the company" litigation and cases involving financial fraud) was an outstanding platform for the focus of her current law practice, which is handling "the harder" (some might say nasty) divorce and family law cases where something very important or valuable is often at issue.

In all cases, Ashley's goal is to obtain a favorable result for clients as quickly and efficiently as possible so they can move on to the life they desire and deserve to be living. She strongly believes in resolution focused and strategic litigation (which means that she will counsel a client to litigate when it needs to be done, for example to align an unruly spouse more with legal reality when they are taking a ridiculous position) but believes resolving matters out of court is usually in the best interest of the clients, not only financially, but also psychologically.

Outside of the office, and spending time with our young children, Ashley's passion is animal rescue, and trying to make the world a better place with kindness to animals. Ashley also enjoys horseback riding, mountain biking, snowboarding, tennis, photography, theater, and a variety of other activities. Ashley is married to Christopher R. Bruce, and can be reached at (561) 810-0170 or abruce@brucepa.com.

 **Christopher R. Bruce** is a divorce lawyer and appellate lawyer for divorce cases and has been for nearly all of his legal career and he is a Florida Bar Board Certified Marital & Family Law Specialist. His law practice is predominately limited to representing his

South Florida clients in divorce and family court matters involving business valuation and asset tracing issues, the need to confront a difficult or intimidating person, the prosecution or defense of long-term financial support claims, or serious issues involving children.

Chris takes a particular interest in representing women in divorces from narcissistic or emotionally abusive/manipulative husbands. This is because Chris feels these cases are most likely to result in his client having a dramatically improved and transformed-for-the-better life once the divorce is over.

Chris founded the Bruce Law Firm, P.A. in November 2016 and the multi-lawyer law firm is limited to divorce and family law matters.

Chris is a native of Palm Beach County, Florida, and a graduate of Palm Beach Gardens High School. Outside of the office, and spending time with his family, his passion is saltwater fishing and marine conservation. Chris enjoys participating in South Florida billfish tournaments and promoting marine species and habitat conservation.

Chris frequently publishes articles on current topics in Florida Divorce Law, and serves as a resource to news agencies reporting on Florida divorce issues. His articles have appeared in the *South Florida Daily Business Review, Palm Beach County Bar Bulletin* and several other Florida Bar publications.

A proponent of keeping families together, Chris developed **www.StayMarriedFlorida.com**, a resource for helping people build, have, and keep happy and healthy relationships.

Chris developed **www.BrucePA.com** to further help people create the best probability for making their divorce a *"Best Divorce"* that allows them to move on to a life to be proud of when their divorce is over. The website's resources include complementary books, seminars, and forums on divorce strategy, law, and procedure.

If you would like to contact Chris in regard to appearing on StayMarriedFlorida.com, a Florida divorce or family law matter, this book, or anything else, you can call (561) 810-0170 or send an email to cbruce@brucepa.com.

Made in the USA
Monee, IL
08 August 2023

40615395R00073